# Larry's GARDEN LOT

HAPPY

**Robson Books**

First published in Great Britain in 1988 by Robson Books Ltd,
Bolsover House 5 – 6 Clipstone Street, London W1P 7EB.

**British Library Cataloguing in Publication Data**

Larry
  Larry's garden lot.
  Rn: Terence Parkes I. Title
  741.5'942

ISBN 0-86051-489-7

Printed in Great Britain by Billing & Sons Ltd, Worcester

PARAFFIN

BROWN  GREEN  CLEAR

BOTTLE
GARDEN

LAKELAND LTD
GARDEN POOLS
THE
WINDERMERE

HORTICULTURAL PURSUIT